T0266636

GEORGIA CHRISTOU

Georgia is a previous member of the Royal Court Young Writers' Group. *Yous Two* was shortlisted for the Verity Bargate Award in 2015. It is her first full-length play.

She is on commission to Paines Plough and the HighTide Escalator Plays.

She has also been selected as part of Channel 4's 4Stories scheme and is writing an original single drama which will shoot in 2018.

Georgia Christou

YOUS TWO

NICK HERN BOOKS

London

www.nickhernbooks.co.uk

A Nick Hern Book

Yous Two first published in Great Britain as a paperback original in 2018 by Nick Hern Books Limited, The Glasshouse, 49a Goldhawk Road, London W12 8QP

Yous Two copyright © 2018 Georgia Christou

Georgia Christou has asserted her right to be identified as the author of this work

Cover image: www.istockphoto.com/ASIFE

Designed and typeset by Nick Hern Books, London
Printed in the UK by Mimeo Ltd, Huntingdon, Cambridgeshire PE29 6XX

A CIP catalogue record for this book is available from the British Library

ISBN 978 1 84842 729 7

Yous Two was first performed at Hampstead Theatre Downstairs, London, on 18 January 2018. The cast was as follows:

FUDGE	Ali Barouti
RACHEL	Leah Harvey
BILLIE	Shannon Tarbet
JONNY	Joseph Thompson
Director	Chelsea Walker
Designer	Rosanna Vize
Lighting	Jamie Platt
Sound	George Dennis

Thanks

To Ella Hickson for making me finish the bloody thing.

To DC Jackson and Alison O'Donnell.

To Kara Fitzpatrick and Lisa Foster for taking me on and holding my hand.

To all the actors who were part of development process – Abigail Andjel, Jessica Barden, Calvin Demba, Jessica Ellis, Maddy Hill, Daniel Mays, Lloyd Thomas, Anita-Joy Uwajeh.

To Lyric Hammersmith Young Writers Course, HighTide Theatre and Soho Theatre.

To the wonderful cast and crew at Hampstead Theatre. To Chelsea Walker for your unfaltering belief in the play.

To Andreana, Andy and Mia Christou.

To Hasan.

And to Louis. The biggest feeling I ever...

For my family, of course.

Characters

JONNY, *male, thirty-six*
BILLIE, *female, fifteen*
FUDGE, *male, sixteen*
RACHEL, *female, sixteen*

Note on Text

/ signifies when another character starts talking.

– signifies an interruption.

The play should be played at pace.

The play is set in the south of England but please feel at liberty to place it elsewhere.

This text went to press before the end of rehearsals and so may differ slightly from the play as performed.

Scene One

A bathroom. JONNY, dark features, mid-thirties, lies in the
bath smoking a joint. The door handle goes. He covers himself.

JONNY. Don't come in.

The door opens a tiny bit.

Don't come in I said.

BILLIE (*from off behind the door*). Are you in there?

JONNY. No.

BILLIE. You gonna be long?

JONNY. I don't know.

BILLIE. How long?

JONNY. I don't know I said. I only just got in.

BILLIE. You're smoking.

JONNY. Am I?

BILLIE. In the bath, that's disgusting.

JONNY. I'm allowed. I'm a grown-up.

BILLIE. You'll be all clean with bad breath.

JONNY. Lovely.

BILLIE. It's a nasty habit you know.

JONNY takes a drag. Leaves it on a copy of The Sun *next to*
the bath.

You got bubbles?

JONNY. I didn't put.

BILLIE. I need to go.

JONNY. Hold it. Five minutes, Bill.

BILLIE. I'm desperate.

JONNY. What number?

BILLIE. Just a one.

JONNY. You'll have to wait.

BILLIE. I need a wee. Is it my fault I need a wee? You can't be annoyed at me for needing to go toilet. I should be annoyed at you.

JONNY. Is that right?

BILLIE. If you was a doctor or a lawyer we'd have a house with five bathrooms and I could wee whenever I liked.

Beat.

JONNY. One minute.

Don't come in.

JONNY *runs the tap, pours in half a bottle of Radox, froths the bubbles up while they talk.*

BILLIE. It's early to be in the bath anyway.

JONNY. Just give it a second, I've put bubbles.

BILLIE. Who has a bath a four o'clock?

JONNY. Old people.

BILLIE. You're not old. Not compared to the other dads. Rachel Axdale says her sister thinks you're ten out of ten. She's a massive skank though.

JONNY. Billie!

BILLIE. What? It's true, Dad! She'll do it with anyone and she doesn't even make them bag it up.

JONNY. Don't talk like that it's vile.

BILLIE. She's vile. Rachel said she caught Helen crying in her bedroom the other day and when she looked down on the floor there was green gunk / in her dirty knickers.

JONNY. Behave.

Beat.

Whose knickers?

BILLIE. Helen's obviously. The one who fancies you.

JONNY. Do you really think this conversation is appropriate?

BILLIE. I don't do anything wrong and I get an earful and Helen Axdale's getting all sympathy and thrush cream from her mum. She makes documentaries for Channel 4 though so she's probably quite used to stuff like that.

JONNY. Right.

BILLIE. Did you find anything today?

JONNY. Not really.

BILLIE. Was you looking properly?

JONNY. No I was looking with my eyes closed.

BILLIE. You know what I mean.

JONNY. Don't start.

BILLIE. I'm not.

Beat.

It's just a job won't land in your lap. You need to try a bit.

JONNY. You're trying enough for the both of us.

BILLIE. Rachel's dad works at the university, I could ask him?

JONNY. I haven't got two O levels to rub together, what am I gonna be doing at a university?

BILLIE. They might need cleaners or something.

JONNY. I tore the ligaments in my shoulder, Billie, I can't be scrubbing floors. I've got limited options right now, you know that.

BILLIE. I know. I just worry.

He arranges the bubbles to make sure they cover him.

JONNY. Yeah well leave the worrying to me alright. They're done. (*The bubbles.*)

BILLIE *enters. Small, serious, wears school uniform. She lifts the seat, pees.*

Anyway I have got some good news. I spoke to my claims geezer and he said it could be up to twenty thousand. He's sure we'll get it.

BILLIE. They said that six months ago.

JONNY. These things take time. It'll be worth it though for twenty grand. What shall we do with it? Buy you a car if you want.

BILLIE. We should use it for a deposit. On a house. If you got a proper job we could get a mortgage.

JONNY. You're no fun.

BILLIE. We could though.

JONNY. Don't get all…

BILLIE. What?

JONNY. What we eating tonight?

BILLIE. I think I'll just have a snack.

JONNY. You're not on a diet again?

BILLIE. No.

JONNY. You was a nightmare last time.

BILLIE. I'm not on a diet, Dad.

JONNY. Women are always on diets. They don't work you know.

BILLIE. I know, that's why I'm not on one. I just don't have much time before I go out.

Beat.

JONNY. What do you mean?

She wipes herself, pulls up her knickers. JONNY *averts his eyes. She washes her hands in his bath water.*

BILLIE. I mean I'm going out.

JONNY. Out?

BILLIE. You know out, Dad. Beyond the front / door.

JONNY. It's Friday.

BILLIE. I know.

JONNY. How rude.

BILLIE. What?

JONNY. How rude is that to cancel plans.

BILLIE. Plans are something you write on a calendar... we get takeaway every week.

JONNY. It's EuroMillions. Rollover. Sixty-nine mill. Don't you wanna be here when we win it?

BILLIE. Struck by lightning forty times, Dad. Forty times.

JONNY. You'll be sorry when I run off to Barbados and you're left here doing your homework. Where you going then?

BILLIE. Nowhere.

JONNY. Don't be stupid, Billie, I'm not letting you out if I don't know where you're going.

BILLIE. I won't be back late.

JONNY. Billie.

BILLIE. You'll laugh.

JONNY. Go on. Bills?

BILLIE. It's just this thing. This open-evening thing.

JONNY. For what?

BILLIE. A college.

JONNY. And?

BILLIE. And nothing. I just want to go and have a look.

JONNY. Bloody hell.

BILLIE. I told you you'd laugh.

JONNY. No I just, I thought you was gonna say –

BILLIE. What?

JONNY. Nothing. Looks like rain you know.

BILLIE. Not to me it doesn't.

JONNY. I suppose you want a lift.

BILLIE. Not in the slightest.

JONNY. What's that supposed to mean?

BILLIE. It means I want a lift over my dead body.

JONNY. Snob.

BILLIE. I've told you. I'm not getting in the car till you've sorted the window.

JONNY. And I told you a new window's a hundred and fifty quid.

BILLIE. So there we are then.

JONNY. It's not private, this school? Is it?

BILLIE. –

JONNY. Cos there's no way we could –

BILLIE. I could get a scholarship, for my Maths.

JONNY. Billie, it ain't that big school on top of the hill?

BILLIE. I bet hardly anyone applies on Maths.

JONNY. You're not serious?

BILLIE. Why not?

JONNY. It's a boarding school.

BILLIE. So?

JONNY. What's wrong with your school? It's not that, it's all the stuff that goes with it – the uniform, hockey sticks, all that.

BILLIE. I just wanna look.

JONNY. I'll take you but –

BILLIE. I don't need you to take me.

BILLIE *exits*.

JONNY *is still, watches the door for a moment. He takes a bar of soap, stretches to soap his back. He lets out a cry of pain.*

Drys his hands on the carpet, finds and relights the joint. He tries again to reach his back, bangs on the side of the bath.

(*Offstage.*) What now?

You alright?

JONNY. –

BILLIE. That stinks.

She re-enters.

JONNY. It's medicinal. My shoulder.

BILLIE. Is that it?

JONNY. I can't reach.

BILLIE. –

JONNY. Could you…?

A beat before she goes and sits behind him.

He hands her the soap. She rubs it over his neck and back.

BILLIE. You've got a spot.

JONNY. Don't touch it.

BILLIE. There's all blackheads.

JONNY. Told you, I can't reach.

Silence for a moment as she washes him.

BILLIE. Got my predicted grades today.

JONNY. And?

BILLIE. A-star Maths, A-star Science –

JONNY. Like we thought.

BILLIE. C for English.

JONNY. Sounds alright?

BILLIE. C's not good enough.

JONNY. They got crystal balls then, these teachers?

BILLIE. It's a prediction. An indication.

JONNY. I don't like that. It means you can't win.

BILLIE. You don't win at exams, Dad, it's not like the Lottery.

JONNY. Ruins the surprise. Like finding out what your baby is before it's born.

BILLIE. I got a B for French which is a joke cos James Perry copied every one of my answers on the mock and he got an A.

JONNY. You don't wanna be French when you grow up, do you?

BILLIE. *Oui*.

JONNY. There we go then. I know you're smart and so do you and that's all that matters.

BILLIE. Not really, Dad. Not if I want to go uni. Or get a good job. Or live in a house with five bathrooms.

Beat.

JONNY. I am trying you know.

BILLIE. I wasn't talking about you.

JONNY. But it isn't that easy.

BILLIE. I didn't say it was.

JONNY. Do you want for anything?

BILLIE. Yeah. Loads of stuff.

JONNY. In your life have I ever let you go without?

BILLIE. I just said. Yes.

JONNY. You're out of order, do you know that?

BILLIE. Don't project your insecurities on me.

JONNY. You think I'm making it up?

BILLIE. I don't wanna –

JONNY. It's uncertain times, Billie, with the economy.

BILLIE. Okay.

JONNY. Don't you read the papers?

BILLIE. Do you?

JONNY. We're in a transition stage.

BILLIE. I get it. Stop going on.

JONNY. Who's going on? You're the one who come in bleating
    on about Cs and Bs. Heaven forbid I get five minutes' peace
    on my own.

BILLIE. I've been in school all day. Five minutes alone. Please
    god, / just give me five minutes so I can sit and write my
    diary like a massive princess.

JONNY. You have no respect. You show no respect for anyone.

BILLIE. Relax, Doris. I've got to leave in a minute anyway.
    What you doing?

JONNY. Forget it. There you go, I'm getting out, you spoiled
    it now.

JONNY stands up in the bath with his back to BILLIE. *He
covers his bits with his hands.*

I just wanted to do one thing for myself and you had to ruin
it for me. Pass me my...

She flings him the towel. It drops into the bath behind him.

Goodness' sake.

*He bends to grab it, still covering his genitals with one hand
then wraps the towel round his lower half.*

BILLIE. Oh my god.

JONNY. Everything's hard work with you.

BILLIE. Dad!

JONNY. You came in looking for a fight.

He climbs out of the bath.

BILLIE. Dad, you got something on your bottom.

*He puts shaving foam on his face and shaves with a razor
which is on the sink.*

It's like a growth. On, round your bottom, I saw something.

JONNY. What?

BILLIE. Like coming… out. / Cancer. It might be cancer.

JONNY. What d'you mean coming / out?

BILLIE. I've seen it in biology. Cancer of the colon. Your bum hole swells and you get little growths.

JONNY. I've not got cancer, Billie. I have piles thank you for noticing.

BILLIE. Mr Minns said it happens all the time – they see the blood, think it's piles and then bang – three months later they're wearing a head scarf and doing charity bike rides.

JONNY. Your teacher said that?

BILLIE. You have to go up A&E, Dad.

JONNY. Why do you say these things?

BILLIE. I mean it. I'll worry otherwise.

JONNY. Let's not fall out.

BILLIE. You never go when I ask you.

JONNY. You're a scaremongerer.

BILLIE. We've been lucky up till now but one day it'll happen. I'll come home and find you dead, blood leaking from your bumhole and a cat licking it up. I don't need that right in the middle of exams, Dad.

JONNY. We don't have a cat.

BILLIE. Don't joke.

JONNY. But we *don't*.

BILLIE. Will you go doctor's or not?

JONNY. Not.

BILLIE. Then I'm gonna have to look.

Beat.

JONNY. No way.

BILLIE. It's me or the doctor's.

JONNY. You must be joking.

BILLIE. What did I just say about taking me serious?

JONNY. I do / take you serious.

BILLIE. You know how you feel about hospitals.

JONNY. I'll go tomorrow.

BILLIE. Liar. Bend down again.

JONNY. Get out of it.

BILLIE. Just for a second.

JONNY. Enough now.

He faces her, razor in hand.

BILLIE. I'll know when I see, I'll remember it from science.

JONNY. What is wrong with you?

BILLIE. I have to look, Dad, before I go out.

JONNY. Maybe you'd better stay in.

BILLIE. Come on.

JONNY. Monitor me.

BILLIE. Let's get it over with.

JONNY. We can have Chinese if you like?

BILLIE. No, Dad. Now.

She tugs the towel hard.

The towel drops. There is moment, a fraction of stillness before JONNY snatches his towel up. He covers himself. He throws the razor in the sink.

JONNY. You know maybe I was wrong, maybe predictions are good. Cos God knows I'd have run a fucking mile if I'd known it was you coming out.

He exits, the shaving foam still on his face.

BILLIE (*shouting*). Potty mouth.

She pulls the plug in the bath.

Shall we get them to deliver? Dad?

The sound of rain.

Scene Two

BILLIE *and* RACHEL. RACHEL *is lying down with her leg propped up on* BILLIE*'s lap who is sitting on the edge of the bath.* RACHEL *is holding a pot of hot wax up whilst* BILLIE *smears it onto* RACHEL*'s legs with a stick.*

RACHEL. I told them. Anna, Dave, you're acting like a pair of fucking mugs.

BILLIE. Bet that helped.

RACHEL. I said you've ruined my sixteenth so I hope that plays on your conscience for the rest of your life. They really drag me down d'you know that. That's too –

BILLIE. Sorry.

RACHEL. Need to let it cool –

BILLIE. Yeah sorry.

RACHEL. I mean tell me if you think I was out of order. Was I?

BILLIE. –

RACHEL. They keep saying they just want me to be happy. We just want you to be happy, Rachel. Well clearly they don't as they literally hold the keys to my happiness and they won't hand them over. Keisha had a house party. Rahima had a house party.

BILLIE. How's that?

RACHEL. Like skin meltingly hot. Whatever just let's just...

BILLIE. I don't know why you don't just shave them.

RACHEL. They're too hairy.

BILLIE. They wouldn't be if you shaved them.

RACHEL. It'll last longer.

BILLIE. It's gonna hurt.

RACHEL. Have you had it done?

BILLIE. No, but I know it will hurt.

RACHEL. It can't be that bad.

BILLIE. Ready?

RACHEL. Yeah.

BILLIE. Okay. Take a deep breath in –

RACHEL. Just rip it off quick –

> BILLIE *rips the wax strip off.*

> Fuck! Billie, I wasn't ready.

BILLIE. I told you.

RACHEL. Is it bleeding?

BILLIE. Course not.

JONNY (*from off*). You alright up there?

BILLIE *and* RACHEL. Yeah.

BILLIE. We're fine, Dad.

> *Beat.*

> You can't scream like that every time.

RACHEL. It hurt.

BILLIE. Should have done this at yours.

RACHEL. Lock the door.

BILLIE. Doesn't have one.

RACHEL. I love this place. It's proper old-school.

BILLIE. Proper shit you mean. Ready?

RACHEL. Oh my god I don't know if I can handle any more.

BILLIE. Take a deep breath like I said.

RACHEL. I need an anaesthetic.

BILLIE. Like you're giving birth.

RACHEL. Can I have a break?

BILLIE. We only just –

RACHEL. Two minutes.

BILLIE. You need to look at my English before you go as well remember.

RACHEL. I'm not in a hurry.

BILLIE. I didn't tell my dad you was staying for dinner.

RACHEL. It's fine. I had like four bags of crisps at lunch anyway. Just give me two minutes to mentally prepare.

BILLIE. Your feet smell like dead rats by the way.

RACHEL. Don't.

RACHEL sits up. Lifts a foot to her face and smells it.

Beat.

I'll give them a quick...

RACHEL sits on the edge of the bath where BILLIE *was sat. She runs a little water in the bath, paddles her feet in and soaps them through the conversation.*

How old is he? Your dad?

BILLIE. Thirty-six.

RACHEL. Mate. My da– Dave's nearly sixty. He could be your granddad.

BILLIE. I haven't seen him in ages.

RACHEL. He's at work most of the time, hiding from my mum. She basically hates him.

BILLIE. What did he do?

RACHEL. Nothing bad. Mostly he just sits in his office. Listening to songs about, like war and stuff. And crying into his coffee. Anna calls him an island.

BILLIE. –

RACHEL. Like hard to reach. She keeps coming into my bedroom to 'hang out' and watch me get changed. She goes, 'It's nothing I haven't seen before, you came out my front bum.'

BILLIE laughs.

She's a proper pervert. My sister's the same. She's like Mum
and I'm like Dad. I mean, you're always gonna turn into one
of your parents aren't you, it's just about choosing the one
who's slightly less mental.

Beat.

Shit. Sorry.

BILLIE. For what?

RACHEL. You know.

BILLIE. Oh. Don't be. My dad says she was a selfish cow so
I didn't miss out on much.

RACHEL. Still.

BILLIE. Honestly. I'm not emotionally scarred or anything.
I don't remember her so...

RACHEL. Well, sorry anyway.

BILLIE. Gimme your leg. And you can't scream okay?

RACHEL. I'll try. But I can't make any promises.

Beat.

How come he's always around, your dad? Does he work
nights?

BILLIE. He works from home. Mostly.

RACHEL. Doing what?

BILLIE. Like, freelance stuff.

RACHEL. Doing what though?

BILLIE. It's sort of...

RACHEL. What?

BILLIE. Like a sales thing.

RACHEL. Billie?

BILLIE. Yeah.

RACHEL. Is your dad a dealer?

BILLIE. No!

RACHEL. I wouldn't say anything.

BILLIE. He isn't.

RACHEL. He smokes weed though.

BILLIE. I dunno.

RACHEL. I could smell it soon as we walked in. Do you think
he'd sell me some?

BILLIE. He's not a dealer.

RACHEL. Okay.

Beat.

BILLIE. Rachel!

RACHEL. What?

BILLIE. He's not –

RACHEL. I won't tell anyone.

BILLIE. He sells tickets.

RACHEL. Tickets?

BILLIE. Like football, gigs, that sort of thing.

RACHEL. Amazing.

BILLIE. He needs to get a proper job.

RACHEL. Does he give you any?

BILLIE. I never ask.

RACHEL. What can he get?

BILLIE. I dunno. I don't ask, I said.

RACHEL. My dad is so desperate to go to the Arsenal game
next week.

BILLIE. Is that a hint?

RACHEL. No.

BILLIE. Good.

RACHEL. Actually it was.

BILLIE. I'll ask but –

RACHEL. Please. Mum's having a life-drawing party that night. Some naked hippy comes and leaves their crusty old pubes on our sofa and we have to like paint them or whatever. The last one had the biggest nipples I've ever seen I swear. Like a giant owl watching me across the living room.

BILLIE. Do you think if I got him the tickets, he'd do some tutoring with me? On my English.

RACHEL. I dunno. Maybe.

BILLIE. Would you ask?

RACHEL. You only need a C. As long as you don't have to retake who gives a shit?

BILLIE. C's not good enough.

RACHEL. I'm not predicted anything above a C.

BILLIE. I just mean, for where I wanna go –

RACHEL. I'm dropping as many subjects as I can. I'm just gonna do music and art. Doss classes.

BILLIE. What about uni?

RACHEL. I'm gonna go travelling instead, take a load of drugs, have sex with some Australians. That's what my parents did. It's how they met.

BILLIE. Your dad's not Australian.

RACHEL. You don't marry them, you just have sex with them.

BILLIE. By time you get back I'll be nearly qualified, you can get some free counselling.

RACHEL. I won't need counselling.

BILLIE. We need to finish your legs.

RACHEL. Mate, can't we do it in your room, it's boiling in here?

BILLIE. You'll get wax all on my sheets. Look at my essay while I do it.

RACHEL. Bet you'd be allowed a party, wouldn't you.

BILLIE. Why?

RACHEL. No reason.

BILLIE. Do you reckon your dad would look over my coursework as well?

RACHEL. Dunno. Maybe for a –

BILLIE *pulls off the strip*, RACHEL *screams*.

Fuck!

Scene Three

Dead of night. FUDGE *stumbles into the bathroom fully clothed, bare feet. He doesn't turn the light on. Lifts the lid, stands, pissing.* JONNY, *in just his boxers, opens the bathroom door, switches on the light.*

JONNY. What, who the / fuck –

FUDGE. Shit. Sorry, man, I'm just –

JONNY *runs offstage*.

Shit.

JONNY *re-enters, holding a baseball bat*.

JONNY. What do you think you're doing / in my –

FUDGE. Listen, I'm –

JONNY. Think you're a big man, breaking in my house –

FUDGE. No, man, I ain't, I didn't break in. I'm just, I'm staying over / I didn't break in.

JONNY. You think I'm an idiot? / Some kind of idiot?

FUDGE. Course I, please please put that down. And put some clothes on, bruv.

JONNY. 'Bruv'–

FUDGE. Sir, I meant sir.

JONNY. Tell me what to do in my own house?

FUDGE. No, sir.

JONNY. In my own fucking house. Try it. Try it you melt. If I want to slap your melt face with my nuts I will, / 'bruv', cos we're in my house now.

FUDGE. Fuck.

BILLIE (*offstage*). Oi, what's goin' on?

JONNY. Do you understand me? Not your brother, mate, not me. Peasant. Fucking peasants, the lot of you. Thought you'd stop for a piss –

FUDGE. No.

JONNY. You think I'm a cunt –

FUDGE. No. Shit. You've got it wrong, man. Put that down. Please, I'm here I'm here with Billie –

JONNY rushes at FUDGE, smashes his head against the wall, grabs his throat.

BILLIE enters.

BILLIE. Oh my god, Dad.

FUDGE. Please –

JONNY. Are you alright, Billie?

BILLIE. Dad, get off him.

JONNY. Did he hurt you?

BILLIE. Dad, no, get off him, what are you doing?

JONNY. Go to bed, Billie.

BILLIE. Dad, he's / my friend.

JONNY. Go to bed, babe. You don't have to be scared, / I'll sort it, go to bed, baby.

BILLIE goes to JONNY tries to pulls him off FUDGE.

BILLIE. Let go of him. You'll kill him, he's my friend, I know him. He's my friend.

JONNY lets go of FUDGE's neck.

Beat.

Put it down, Daddy.

JONNY *holds tight to the bat.*

My god, what… Put something on, Dad.

JONNY *doesn't move.*

Here.

*She takes off her bathrobe, shivering, stands in her shorts
and a strappy top.* JONNY *stares at her for a moment.*

Takes the bathrobe, puts it on. Stares at BILLIE, *does not
look at* FUDGE *for the remainder of the scene.*

You're scaring me.

JONNY. You alright?

FUDGE. I think so.

JONNY. Not you.

BILLIE. I'm fine.

JONNY *takes in the state of the room.*

It was Rachel's birthday. I didn't think you'd… I was gonna
tidy up in the morning.

JONNY. Will he be alright?

BILLIE. I dunno.

FUDGE. I think I'm okay.

JONNY. So you two…?

BILLIE. He's my friend. From school. He missed the last bus.
He's sleeping on the floor, I promise.

JONNY. If you're lying to me, Billie…

BILLIE. –

JONNY. If I find out you're looking me in the eye and lying,
Billie, I swear –

FUDGE. Please, man, I'm sorry I just want to go home.

BILLIE. Shut up.

JONNY. If I go in that bedroom I'm gonna find a bed all made
up on the floor, am I?

BILLIE. –

JONNY. Am I?

BILLIE. I didn't think you'd be back till the morning. I was gonna tell you then.

JONNY. I asked you a question, Billie.

BILLIE. –

JONNY. You've never been a liar. You're a lot of other things but... Not to me. Do you understand?

BILLIE. Yes.

JONNY. Is he sleeping in your bed?

BILLIE. Yes.

> JONNY *drops the baseball bat.* FUDGE *flinches at the sound of it hitting the floor.*

JONNY. Are you –

BILLIE. Oh my god. No.

JONNY. –

BILLIE. I said no, Dad. We're not... Stop looking at me like that.

> *Beat.*

> JONNY *exits.*

> *Long pause.*

FUDGE. Is that your dad then?

BILLIE. –

FUDGE. He seems nice.

> *Blackout.*

Scene Four

Christmas Eve. BILLIE *is breathing heavily, kneeling over the toilet.* JONNY *is at the door. She flushes the toilet, slumps against the side of the bath.*

JONNY. Shall I / come in –

BILLIE. Yeah it's fine.

JONNY *enters. He wears a Santa Claus hat.*

JONNY. Billie, you don't half look pasty.

BILLIE. –

JONNY. Do you think it was that –

BILLIE. Oh shut up.

JONNY. I thought it was done.

BILLIE. It wasn't you.

JONNY. You're gonna be poorly for the big day.

BILLIE. I feel a bit better now.

JONNY. This is why I shouldn't cook.

BILLIE. If it was food poisoning you'd be sick too, wouldn't you. There's a bug going round.

JONNY. Right. So you don't think it was the chicken?

BILLIE. I don't want to think about it, Dad.

JONNY. Right you are. Can I get you anything?

BILLIE. I just wanna sit here.

JONNY. Water?

BILLIE. You're alright.

JONNY. Are you feeling like you might –

BILLIE. No. I just need to sit still.

JONNY. I'll wait downstairs for you then, eh?

BILLIE. Stay with me a minute.

JONNY. Course.

Beat.

You look very young.

BILLIE. Sit with me then.

He hesitates then goes to her. She leans her head on his shoulder.

Daddy?

JONNY. Billie?

BILLIE. Do you ever worry that I might have it too?

JONNY. Have it?

BILLIE. Like her?

JONNY. –

BILLIE. I'm like her, aren't I?

JONNY. Nah.

BILLIE. I am. I know I am. I see how you look at me sometimes.

JONNY. I don't look at you like nothing, you nutter.

BILLIE. Dad!

JONNY. Sorry. Bad choice…

BILLIE. Why are you breathing all funny?

JONNY. I'm not.

BILLIE. I can feel it.

JONNY. You're alright, babe.

BILLIE. Dad?

JONNY. You can call me Santa.

BILLIE. Santa. If you get any more Arsenal tickets, will you –

JONNY. Billie. Don't push it.

BILLIE. Rachel's dad lectures English. If he'd help with my coursework I could bump my mark up.

JONNY. Is this still about that school?

BILLIE. I can't go there now anyway. But if I wanna go to a decent uni –

JONNY. Uni? Slow down / a bit.

BILLIE. Durham, Edinburgh, they all look at your GCSEs.

JONNY. Edinburgh?

BILLIE. I'm not gonna get in anywhere decent with a C, Dad.

JONNY. So you keep saying.

BILLIE. Well, I have to think about these things. Don't I?

JONNY. Yeah fine, I dunno.

BILLIE. Exactly. You don't know.

Beat.

JONNY. I've always done my best by you, Billie. I'm sorry if it's not good enough.

BILLIE. I didn't mean –

JONNY. I've had my injury to deal with as well, remember.

BILLIE. I know you have.

JONNY. The fact is, I can't trust you now.

BILLIE. Dad –

JONNY. How do I know these tickets you want aren't for that kid?

BILLIE. They're not. You could call Rachel's dad yourself.

JONNY. And how would that make me look? Like I don't have a clue what's going on in my own child's life and he can sit down with his wife all la-di-da / and talk about what a horrible mess I'm making of –

BILLIE. They're not like that, Dad, they're really nice.

JONNY. It's not that the two of yous are going out. I know you're gonna want to be hanging around with boys and that but I cannot tolerate you betraying my trust.

BILLIE. You're being melodramatic.

JONNY. Let's not argue. It's my busiest night of the year.

BILLIE. I'm not it's just –

JONNY. This is a pointless conversation anyway. I can't afford to be giving stuff away. He's a professor, he can put his hand in his pocket.

BILLIE. Don't get all cross, / we can't discuss anything without –

JONNY. I'm not 'getting all' anything. Anyway like I said it's pointless. I've had my memberships taken off me.

BILLIE. You what?

JONNY. The clubs have taken them back.

BILLIE. And?

JONNY. And I can't get any more seats obviously.

BILLIE. What about the money you paid?

JONNY. That's it.

BILLIE. You've lost it you mean.

JONNY. Well, they certainly ain't gonna hand it back to me, Billie. I mean I could call up and see if they'll pop a cheque in the post but I think it's more likely they'll have me nicked.

BILLIE. I told you. I told you you needed to pack it in. I told you to get a proper job. How much did you lose?

JONNY. That's none of your –

BILLIE. How much, Dad?

JONNY. Two.

BILLIE. Two hundred? You better say two hundred, Daddy.

JONNY. Two hundred, Daddy.

BILLIE. Honestly?

JONNY. No.

BILLIE. Two thousand pounds. You've lost two thousand pounds? Fucking hell.

JONNY. You watch your language.

BILLIE. Bloody hell, Dad.

JONNY. Did you hear me?

BILLIE. Where did you get that sort of money from in the first place?

JONNY. It's a loan.

BILLIE. Well, how you gonna pay it back if you can't sell the tickets?

JONNY. It doesn't matter, I'll get my payout soon and we can pay it off and forget it.

BILLIE. You need to get a job and start paying back now.

JONNY. Billie, you're the kid and I'm the grown-up, right? I think I'm better qualified to deal with this than you are, / do you understand?

BILLIE. Well obviously not as you appear to have lost TWO THOUSAND POUNDS. I've told you how many times, Dad, what if you'd gone prison?

BILLIE lunges at JONNY and buries her head in his chest. There is a beat before he puts his arms around her and strokes her hair.

JONNY. I'm not going prison, you doughnut.

BILLIE. What we gonna do?

JONNY. I'll sort it. I know it's not ideal –

BILLIE. You got that right –

JONNY. You need to relax. Trust me, alright? Madam? I'm Santa remember. Have I ever let you down before?

BILLIE. I won't answer that.

JONNY. Got yourself all worked up –

BILLIE. Can I sit in your legs?

JONNY. I don't wanna catch it as well, Bills, we wanna be alright for tomorrow.

BILLIE. I'll hold my breath.

JONNY sits with his legs crossed. BILLIE climbs onto him like she is climbing into a nest. She presses a button on his hat, it flashes lights. She sucks her thumb.

JONNY. You're getting a bit big for this.

BILLIE. Am I hurting?

JONNY. Take your thumb out your mouth. You don't want buck teeth.

BILLIE (*with thumb in mouth*). I've been alright so far.

JONNY. Anyway it'll be all sicky.

BILLIE. Good point.

She takes her thumb out her mouth. They sit for a moment in the quiet.

This floor is getting really mank.

JONNY. It's always been mank.

BILLIE. Who puts carpet in a bathroom?

JONNY. Where's your mark?

BILLIE. We're sitting on it.

JONNY. What about when he wanted to gut the bathroom?

BILLIE. I dunno why you said no.

JONNY. No one touches this room. It's where my baby was born.

BILLIE. Maybe if you ask the landlord he might offer to do it again?

JONNY. You were such an ugly baby them first few days.

BILLIE. Thanks.

JONNY. The spit of your mum's dad. I was a bit worried to tell the truth cos he was a right... they both were. 'All about the show', do you know what I mean. When I told them, after I'd found her that day, the first thing he says, no word of a lie, he goes, 'What am I gonna tell the bowls club?' That was it for me then, I wasn't letting you anywhere near them.

BILLIE. It's weird to think she was here. That she's been in this room.

JONNY. You come so quick, Bills, honestly. I thought she'd gone for a wee. Then I find her, bent double in here, white as a sheet. You were nearly out before the cab got here.

BILLIE. Do you think I look like her more? As I'm getting older?

JONNY. You don't look like either of us.

BILLIE. I don't look like the milkman, do I?

Beat.

Joke.

JONNY. Very funny.

BILLIE. It is hereditary you know. Depression and schizophrenia and all them things.

JONNY. Not always.

BILLIE. Yeah. But it can be. You can catch it from a parent or it can like skip a generation like the ginger gene. I learnt it in psychology.

JONNY. What are they filling your head with? When I went it was Geography, Maths, PE, proper subjects.

BILLIE. Don't be like that. It makes you sound old.

JONNY. Everyone's got something now. OCD. Bloody ADAD.

BILLIE. ADHD.

JONNY. See. And the kids are more clued-up than us. When I was at school I was a little shit. That's what I was. That's what they told me I was. And I had to deal with the consequences.

BILLIE. And look how that turned out.

Pause.

I like psychology. It's interesting. We learned about this kid and her parents had locked her in a room all her life and had told her things the wrong way round, like they taught her that a chair was called an apple and a table was called a tree. When they found her, the Social Services or whoever, she couldn't talk to anyone. They couldn't understand a word she was saying. They tried to teach her again, make her learn the words, but she couldn't… She just stopped talking altogether in the end. It was too confusing I suppose. I cried when I watched the film.

JONNY *shifts*.

JONNY. Move your head a minute.

He is sweating slightly.

BILLIE. How could you do that to a little baby though. I think that's even worse than what my mum did, don't you?

Are you alright?

JONNY. Yeah I'm just feeling a bit... I'm wondering about that chicken?

BILLIE. I told you it's a bug.

JONNY. It did have a bit of a smell.

BILLIE. Don't start.

JONNY. Now I think of it.

BILLIE. You haven't got food poisoning, Dad.

JONNY. That's the thing about a Ruby. That's why they made them in the first place, cover up the smell of bad meat.

Is it hot in here or what?

BILLIE. It's always hot in here.

JONNY. Maybe I've got it too?

BILLIE. You'd know if you did.

JONNY. Yeah that's what I mean, I don't feel right.

BILLIE. It's me, Dad. I need looking after. There's nothing wrong with you. You're meant to be the parent, you're meant to be the one –

JONNY crawls to the toilet. Crouches over it. Deep breaths.

JONNY. Just give us a minute?

BILLIE. Fuck's sake, there's nothing wrong with you.

JONNY. Language, Billie –

BILLIE. There's. Nothing. Wrong –

JONNY retches. Dry.

What are you doing?

JONNY. I'm ill.

BILLIE. You're not. I know you're not. It's all in your head.

JONNY. I'm not going hospital, / I can tell you that now –

BILLIE. You don't need to. It's just in your head, Dad. It feels
real but it isn't.

  JONNY *retches. Dry again. He is shaking.*

JONNY. Oh god –

BILLIE. You're unfair. This is so unfair. You're the nutter.

JONNY. I need a glass of water.

BILLIE. I've got no chance. With you and her. I'll be in
a straitjacket –

JONNY. Can you get me a water please?

BILLIE. YOU'RE NOT SICK, YOU PYSCHO!

  He dry retches again.

  I'm pregnant.

  Beat.

  There's no bug. Nothing wrong with your korma. I've been
  sick all week in school. I'm pregnant, Dad.

  JONNY *turns to the toilet. Pukes his guts up.* BILLIE
  *watches for a second. She takes the hat from his head, rubs
  his back gently. Blackout.*

Scene Five

New Year's Eve. BILLIE *sits on the toilet with a pregnancy test.* FUDGE *stands watching her at a distance. A plastic bag in the middle of them. The taps are running.*

FUDGE. Well?

BILLIE. Just…

FUDGE. What?

BILLIE. Give it a second.

FUDGE. Come on, Billie, man.

BILLIE. I'm trying.

FUDGE. Don't try, relax.

BILLIE. You're not being very relaxing.

FUDGE. Have some juice.

BILLIE. I don't want any of your nasty orange juice, / this is completely unnecessary –

FUDGE. It's Rubicon Mango and it is fucking necessary, Billie.

BILLIE. I thought you wanted to talk?

FUDGE. We can talk after.

BILLIE. Turn away.

FUDGE *tuts.*

I can't do it with your hawky eyes on me.

FUDGE. Hawky?

BILLIE. Just look the other way.

FUDGE. Not hawky.

BILLIE. Oh my god.

FUDGE. Caramel, mate.

BILLIE. Do you want me to go or what?

He turns around.

Pause.

FUDGE. This is long, man. Adele's gonna be pissed.

BILLIE. I'm sure she'll get over it.

FUDGE. She's gonna freeze.

BILLIE. Well, you shouldn't have brought her.

FUDGE. She's family.

BILLIE. So?

FUDGE. So we stick together.

Beat.

Making me late.

BILLIE. For what?

FUDGE. It's New Year's Eve, Billie. I got plans.

BILLIE *pulls her knickers up. Turns the taps off.*

What you doing?

BILLIE. It's a waste of water.

FUDGE. I've don't have time for this. I got to walk her, give her a bath, get myself ready –

BILLIE. The dog goes in the bath?

FUDGE. She has sensitive skin. Eczema.

The sound of a firework, off. The dog starts barking relentlessly.

BILLIE. You need to shut her up.

FUDGE. She's scared.

BILLIE. People will start complaining.

FUDGE. She don't like loud noises. Let me bring her in.

BILLIE. My dad's allergic.

FUDGE. He's not even here.

BILLIE. The hair hurts his eyes.

FUDGE. It's fucking minus-ten out there, Billie. Not that you'd know that in here.

BILLIE. Take your coat off.

FUDGE. I told you I'm not staying.

BILLIE. And I told you, this is a waste of time. I did two tests last week.

FUDGE. Another one won't hurt then, will it?

The barking stops.

BILLIE. See. She's fine.

FUDGE. Probably dead. Drink the juice at least.

She takes a sip. Spits it in the sink.

Billie!

BILLIE. That is rank.

FUDGE. Tramp.

BILLIE. It's all thick.

FUDGE. You can give me the money for this stuff then.

FUDGE *throws the bag at her.*

BILLIE. Oi.

She throws it back at him.

FUDGE. Two pregnancy tests, one carton of juice and a Boost. You owe me / fifteen quid.

BILLIE. I don't think so.

FUDGE. Don't be tight, Billie.

BILLIE. I never asked you to / buy that stuff.

FUDGE. Fifteen quid.

BILLIE. Take it back to the shop.

FUDGE. You can have the Boost as a gift but the rest –

The dog starts barking again.

FUDGE *lets out a frustrated growl. Punches the wall.*

BILLIE. Why d'you do that for?

FUDGE. Look what you made me do.

BILLIE. There's a mark.

FUDGE. You're stressing me out.

BILLIE. I swear, why are boys always doing that?

FUDGE. You either do that test or you give me fifteen pounds.

BILLIE. You better hope my dad don't notice.

FUDGE. Are you listening, Billie?

BILLIE. I'm listening, Fudge.

FUDGE. They're your options. So just… think on them.

BILLIE. You've hurt your hand, haven't you?

FUDGE. No.

BILLIE. Do you want me to look at it?

FUDGE. I'm fine, move from me.

> *Beat.*

> My cousin says if you actually are, then you have to do a DNA test.

BILLIE. Is your cousin Jeremy Kyle?

FUDGE. Funny.

BILLIE. What d'you mean 'if I actually am'?

FUDGE. I dunno.

BILLIE. You think I'm making it up? That's why –

FUDGE. Girls lie to trap good men, Billie.

BILLIE. Your cousin tell you that too?

FUDGE. So what if he did?

> *She takes the test and sits back down.*

BILLIE. Your cousin's a dickhead. Just so you know.

> *Takes a deep breath. Closes her eyes.*

> *Pause.*

> *The sound of her weeing.* FUDGE *looks away. He looks out the window.*

FUDGE. She keeps scratching. Her skin's gonna get sore.

BILLIE. Here.

FUDGE. What?

BILLIE. You wanted to see.

FUDGE. I ain't touching that. And wash your hands.

Beat.

How long –

BILLIE. Was quick last time.

She opens the chocolate bar and eats it on the loo.

FUDGE. How long's it been?

BILLIE. I dunno. Thirty seconds.

FUDGE. Should I time it?

BILLIE. A watched pot.

FUDGE. What?

BILLIE. Never mind.

Pause.

You finished your Geography?

FUDGE. Don't be silly.

BILLIE. It's due in first day back.

FUDGE. I'll do it tomorrow.

BILLIE. Have you even started?

FUDGE. I been busy.

BILLIE. Fudge.

FUDGE. We got family over. I had to share my room with my auntie.

BILLIE. It counts towards our final mark, you know.

FUDGE. I can't sleep, she snores like a donkey. Plus I have to take Adele out four times a day. She had a accident the first day they got here and my cousin kicked her. Cunt.

BILLIE. Told you.

FUDGE. Different cousin.

BILLIE. How many you got?

FUDGE. Too many I swear. There was twenty-six of us
    Christmas Day.

BILLIE. Where d'you all sit?

FUDGE. Least it's quiet here.

BILLIE. You can stay for a bit if you want? Not like… The roof's
    flat upstairs, you get a proper good view of the fireworks, me
    and my dad always… we took a sofa up one year.

FUDGE. Where is he now then?

BILLIE. Out.

FUDGE. Is he coming back?

BILLIE. You scared?

FUDGE. Yeah. Are you not?

BILLIE. Your hand's bruising already.

FUDGE. Yeah. My knife hand as well. Meant to have a trial
    shift at Pelham Saturday.

BILLIE. Should have thought that through.

    BILLIE *looks in the bathroom cabinet, finds a cream.*

FUDGE. Head chef there's proper tapped. If you don't work
    fast enough he throws hot pans at you.

BILLIE. That can't be true.

    He puts out his hand. She rubs the cream in.

FUDGE. What I heard. Is it done?

BILLIE. What?

FUDGE. The test.

BILLIE. Oh. Yeah.

FUDGE. And?

BILLIE. Thought you wanted to look yourself.

FUDGE. What does it say?

BILLIE. It says I'm pregnant. Obviously.

FUDGE. You sure?

BILLIE. Course. The cross means…

FUDGE. –

BILLIE. Told you I wasn't lying.

   Beat.

FUDGE. This is your fault.

BILLIE. Sorry?

FUDGE. You did this on purpose.

BILLIE. Got pregnant on / purpose?

FUDGE. I'm cursed.

BILLIE. Drama queen.

FUDGE. This face. Women see me and they want my genes.

BILLIE. Because you're so modest?

FUDGE. No, dickhead, cos I'm good looking. You told anyone?

BILLIE. Course I –

FUDGE. My parents can't find out.

BILLIE. You're not gonna tell them?

FUDGE. Shut up, they'll kill me. Like I'll actually die. Anyways, my mum don't believe in abortion. You told your dad?

BILLIE. –

FUDGE. Billie!

BILLIE. He found out.

FUDGE. Right, then I'm gonna die anyway. What did he say?

BILLIE. Nothing.

FUDGE. Did he mention me?

BILLIE. No, I mean literally nothing. He hasn't said a word. Not for a week.

FUDGE. Good. That's good.

BILLIE. Is it?

FUDGE. I have to go.

BILLIE. Don't you want to watch the fireworks?

FUDGE. I told you, Adele doesn't like loud noises.

BILLIE. We need to meet before term starts again.

FUDGE. I don't need your help.

BILLIE. To talk about what we're gonna do.

    FUDGE *goes to exit.*

    You said family sticks together.

FUDGE. You're not my family, Billie.

    He exits.

BILLIE. I wasn't talking about me.

    The sounds of fireworks. The dog barks.

Scene Six

The bathroom. BILLIE *is screwing a lock into the door.*

JONNY. You can't be serious.

BILLIE. I am.

JONNY. Am I hearing this right?

BILLIE. You tell me.

JONNY. You want me to evict you?

BILLIE. Yes. Please.

JONNY. So you can move into a B&B?

BILLIE. Just for a bit.

JONNY. With a load of scagheads and mongs.

BILLIE. Don't be unkind, that's a horrible word –

JONNY. Leave that. (*The lock.*)

BILLIE. It'll only take a minute.

JONNY. You're naive. You're being really naive, Billie, if you think it's that easy.

BILLIE. I can manage a hammer and nail, Dad.

JONNY. Not that. The other thing.

BILLIE. I never said it was easy, I'm just thinking about the long term and what's best / for all of us.

JONNY. You've got no idea.

BILLIE. You won't even notice I'm gone.

JONNY. Is that right?

BILLIE. We've barely spoke lately anyway, so…

Beat.

JONNY. That's not true.

BILLIE. I know you're cross –

JONNY. I'm not / cross.

BILLIE. Then why won't you speak to me?

JONNY. I'm speaking to you now.

BILLIE. You can't even look me in the eye.

JONNY. See, you're just saying things now. Making up stories / in your head…

BILLIE. You think I should have –

JONNY. No. No course not.

BILLIE. We're not like that, Dad. Are we?

Beat.

It'll be better for you anyway. Can have some birds round.

JONNY. Yeah, you see if it's better when you've got some bloke banging on your door at three in the morning, you see if it's better when the baby's sick all the time from the damp –

BILLIE. You don't half exaggerate.

JONNY. Alright. You see. You wait and see what it's like. Obviously you know much more than I do.

BILLIE. I don't want to do it... you just have to be a bit desperate or they won't give you somewhere.

JONNY. You aren't desperate. We aren't desperate, we're fine.

BILLIE. Dad –

JONNY. And how does that make me look? If I kick you out. I would never –

BILLIE. It will be worth it if I get a flat.

JONNY. What's wrong with here? I'll get the papering done and that. We can paint your room make a little nursery bit in the corner.

BILLIE. It'll never happen.

JONNY. That's unfair.

BILLIE. Three months. Three months I've been asking you to put a lock on this door.

JONNY. I was gonna do it tomorrow.

BILLIE. You would never have done it.

JONNY. We've managed this long without, what's the hurry?

BILLIE. Everyone has a lock on the bathroom.

JONNY. Is that what all this is about? You're making a point? Alright I get it, point made.

BILLIE. It's not that.

JONNY. We're alright together. Aren't we?

BILLIE. Of course.

JONNY. We have a laugh.

BILLIE. I don't need a laugh, Dad, I need a place to live.

JONNY. YOU HAVE SOMEWHERE TO LIVE.

Beat.

You live here, babe. Nothing's changed, you can stay here till you're a hundred if you want to. That's the point of this place.

BILLIE. But once the baby comes we're gonna need more space.

JONNY. I'll sleep in the living room.

BILLIE. It'll keep you up all night.

JONNY. Don't tell me, Billie. I've done it, remember. I know you think you're Bertie-big-bollocks now cos you've managed to get yourself... but you don't realise. You don't have a clue how hard this will be.

BILLIE. You managed.

JONNY. He won't change his mind, Billie.

Beat.

BILLIE. I know.

JONNY. He's said he doesn't want anything to do with it. You knew that when you made your decision.

BILLIE. I know.

JONNY. Don't go thinking when it's born, when he sees the pictures up on Insta whatever, that he'll come knocking on the door ready to play happy families. It's not going to happen, I can tell you that now.

BILLIE. Alright, I know. I know he won't. But they do say, they say a woman knows how to love her baby as soon as she gets pregnant, it's just an instinct. But a man doesn't, he won't love it until he holds the baby in his arms. They say that. We don't know.

JONNY. He's only a kid himself.

BILLIE. You weren't much older than him when you had me.

JONNY. How do you expect me to sleep at night knowing my grandchild is in some bedsit?

BILLIE. It would only be for a bit, a few months –

JONNY. You're mad if you think it's that easy.

BILLIE. I've spoke to people.

JONNY. Who?

BILLIE. People who've done it before.

JONNY. It's different now, Billie. People did it, we all did it before.

BILLIE. Not everyone.

JONNY. You don't think Mr and Mrs Rachel had their go? Six months on the dole living in some bloody commune. Everyone did it, trust me. We've been rinsed, mate.

BILLIE. You don't know what you're talking about.

JONNY. You thought cos you're knocked up you'll get a flat?

BILLIE. I'll rent somewhere.

JONNY. What you paying with?

BILLIE. I'll get a job.

JONNY. And do your college, and do your uni?

BILLIE. Just because you never did anything.

JONNY. You need to be realistic, Billie.

BILLIE. I'm not an idiot.

JONNY. No, you're a clever bollocks, that's why I didn't want this for you.

BILLIE. I'll say I had to run away. That you beat me up.

JONNY. You've got an imagination on you, I'll give you that.

BILLIE. I should have recorded you swinging that baseball bat around, that would have done it.

JONNY. I was protecting you.

BILLIE. You did a bloody of good job of making sure he never come back.

Beat.

JONNY. Listen, I'm getting my payout soon –

BILLIE. Oh, give it a / rest, Dad –

JONNY. We could move? Maybe even put a little deposit down like you said?

BILLIE. And then what? You gotta have a job to get a mortgage.

JONNY. I'll get a job.

BILLIE. Dad.

JONNY. I know you think I should have done things different.

BILLIE. I don't –

JONNY. No, I know what you think. That I should have
    worked harder and got further and that but I was learning on
    the job with you, Billie, and for everything I've done wrong
    I must have done something right, mustn't I. Cos you're *it*,
    Bill. You're magnificent. It's not true that, what you said.
    I loved you the second I knew about you, the biggest feeling
    I've ever...

    Pause.

    Can I be honest with you? I'm gonna be honest with you
    now okay.

BILLIE. –

JONNY. I'll worry.

BILLIE. I know, Dad, the drug addicts, the Muslims, the –

JONNY. Not that. I mean, I worry about all that stuff, course
    I do, every parent does. But it's more than that with you.

BILLIE. What do you mean?

    Beat.

JONNY. Forget it.

BILLIE. No, go on.

JONNY. I'll say whatever you want.

BILLIE. Go on I said.

JONNY. I don't know what I was thinking. You're nothing
    like her.

    Beat.

BILLIE. Like my mum? Is that what you mean? That I'm like
    my mum?

JONNY. You're a different person. I have to remind myself of that sometimes.

BILLIE. But do you think we're alike?

JONNY. She wasn't well.

BILLIE. That won't happen to me though. Why do you think that would happen to me, I'm nothing like her. Am I?

> JONNY *takes* BILLIE*'s face in his hands, he holds onto it too tight.*

JONNY. Now you listen to me, right. You are not, you'll never be, anything like what she was. And do you know why?

Cos I know. I know you aren't ever gonna leave me.

Scene Seven

Bathroom. JONNY *on a stool.* RACHEL *is shaving the back of* JONNY*'s head with an electric buzzer.*

RACHEL. That okay?

JONNY. Yeah.

RACHEL. I'm not hurting?

JONNY. No, no.

RACHEL. You can tell me if I am.

JONNY. You're alright.

RACHEL. Does it –

JONNY. Ahh.

RACHEL. What, what did I –

JONNY. Got you there.

RACHEL. Jonny!

JONNY. Good actor am I?

RACHEL. Thought I'd chopped your ear off.

JONNY. Bit of a wind-up, me, you'll get used to it.

Beat.

How's it looking?

RACHEL. Yeah.

JONNY. That good, is it?

RACHEL. No, it's… yeah.

JONNY. Right listen, you're hardly filling me with confidence
here.

RACHEL. What time's Billie finishing?

JONNY. Dunno. Midday normally, when she's on an early. Six
o'clock start. She's eight months' pregnant, it takes the
absolute Michael.

RACHEL. Totally.

JONNY. It shouldn't be legal what they're paying her.

RACHEL. She said there's a discount.

JONNY. Fifteen per cent.

RACHEL. That's handy. They've got everything up Asda,
haven't they.

Silence apart from the electric razor.

You nervous?

JONNY. Oh. God yeah. I'm well out of practice, mate. What do
people talk about these days, anyway?

RACHEL. Don't ask me.

JONNY. Come on, I need some tips.

RACHEL. Should ask my sister. She goes on like three dates
a week.

JONNY. She doesn't.

RACHEL. At least.

JONNY. Doing what?

RACHEL. Drinks. Dinner. Trampolining.

JONNY. My first night out with Billie's mum we shared a knickerbocker glory in the Wimpy.

RACHEL. What's Wimpy?

JONNY. Exactly, see. You lot want those metro blokes now isn't it. Soya lattes and leggings.

RACHEL. For some people maybe.

JONNY. Horses for courses?

RACHEL. –

JONNY. Means… not for everyone.

RACHEL. Yeah, no not for everyone. And like even if you think you want that… My mum's really… she doesn't shave her armpits and stuff. But sometimes when my dad's putting his lip balm – he gets really dry… anyway, when he's putting his ChapStick on I see her looking at him like she wishes he was dead.

Pause.

I don't think I'm very good at this.

JONNY. Could have mentioned it earlier.

RACHEL. I think you're done.

JONNY. Like a kipper, mate. Do I wanna look in the mirror or…?

RACHEL. I'd say probably not.

JONNY. Right good so long as I know.

Beat.

He looks in the mirror.

Beat.

He shakes her hand.

RACHEL. What d'you think?

JONNY. Almost as good as that haircut I got off a blind fella that time.

RACHEL. Only cheaper.

JONNY. Only cheaper, that's right.

Beat.

Seriously though, did you want something for –

RACHEL. No!

JONNY. I've got a ten in my coat.

RACHEL. Stop it, no… just shout me a fag and that will do.

JONNY. 'Shout you a fag'?

RACHEL. If that's…

JONNY. Does your mum and dad know you smoke?

RACHEL. They never mention it.

JONNY. Dunno I'd like that myself.

RACHEL. They're not like you.

JONNY. They don't mind?

RACHEL. They don't notice.

Beat.

I think they're probably like nearly done. With each other I mean. Dad's got two phones so…

JONNY. That don't mean –

RACHEL. One of them's full of pictures of this Japanese woman. With her tits out.

JONNY. Right, yeah that does sound… Yeah.

He offers her the packet.

Gotta stay in here though. The boss won't have smoking in the other rooms.

Suicide in slow motion she calls it which is a bit much but that's Bill, isn't it.

He opens the window.

He checks his hair in the mirror.

RACHEL *struggles through the cigarette. She offers him some. He refuses.*

Beat.

Go on then.

Swings on the door frame while he smokes, antsy.

RACHEL. What?

JONNY. Dunno.

RACHEL. What?

JONNY. I feel like a bit of a...

RACHEL. – ?

JONNY. I don't think I should go. To this. Coffee. Thing.

RACHEL. You have to.

JONNY. Don't even drink coffee.

RACHEL. They'll have other drinks.

JONNY. Hot chocolate.

RACHEL. If you want.

JONNY. Would you mind that?

RACHEL. What?

JONNY. If we was on a date and I ordered a hot chocolate?

RACHEL. I wouldn't.

JONNY. She is a real-life grown-up, this Lienne. Works the city, her profile said. Commuter.

RACHEL. So?

JONNY. So what's she want with me?

RACHEL *does a mime – a fisher casting a line.*

Beat.

RACHEL. Fishing.

JONNY. Yeah, very good.

RACHEL. For compliments.

JONNY. I got it.

RACHEL. The thing is it's not about being like the richest or the best looking or whatever.

JONNY. You calling me ugly?

RACHEL. No course I'm –

JONNY. Calling me poor and ugly?

RACHEL. No, I, no –

JONNY. Winding you up again. Warned you.

RACHEL. No, you know what I mean, like... not to be a bitch or anything cos obviously I love her and she's like stunning, but – Billie. For example. She's not like she's the hottest girl in our year or anything. But people just...

JONNY. What?

RACHEL. Okay, like Fudge. He's like one of the... Loads of people would go out with Fudge. He turned down Genevieve from the year above and she's done modelling for M&S so, you know. You're probably just nervous. Because of... Billie said you haven't really been with anyone else since...

JONNY. I've not had much time.

RACHEL. My mum made this documentary. *Suicide and Me: Life After Death*, did you...?

JONNY. Missed that one.

RACHEL. You can still get it on iPlayer... anyway, what came up a lot was it's really common for the people left behind to blame themselves. Like, wondering if they could have done something different or, but the thing is, you couldn't have. And everyone's always saying how well Billie's turned out, all things... My dad's said he'll recommend her. Write a personal letter when we apply to uni.

Pause.

You need to go. Probably. Don't you?

JONNY. Yeah.

RACHEL. Your / date.

JONNY. Yeah no, think I'm gonna give it a swerve actually.

RACHEL. Really?

JONNY. No I don't feel like it so much as it happens. Can hardly go looking like this, can I? He's a big deal then, is he?

RACHEL. Sorry?

JONNY. Your old man. He's got some say in that stuff, unis and…

RACHEL. I dunno.

JONNY. You'll have the pick of the bunch.

RACHEL. I'm not going uni.

JONNY. Early days though, isn't it.

RACHEL. I don't wanna go.

JONNY. Course you do.

RACHEL. Anyway he hasn't offered so…

JONNY. Why d'you think that is?

RACHEL. –

JONNY. Rachel?

RACHEL. I'm not very…

JONNY. What?

RACHEL. I'm in the lower sets for a lot of stuff.

JONNY. So?

RACHEL. So he's probably embarrassed.

JONNY. Never.

RACHEL. You don't know.

JONNY. Or if he is, it won't be for the reason you think.

RACHEL. I'm more like, musical and stuff.

JONNY. Singing?

RACHEL. Kind of.

JONNY. You got a good voice?

RACHEL. I dunno.

JONNY. Go on then.

Beat.

RACHEL. What?

JONNY. Do us a song.

RACHEL. You joking again?

JONNY. Yeah.

RACHEL. Good.

JONNY. Yeah I am.

RACHEL. Cos that would be –

JONNY. Getting the hang of it, aren't you?

RACHEL. Yep.

JONNY. Got the measure of me.

RACHEL. Six foot one.

JONNY. So go on then.

Beat.

One song.

Beat.

RACHEL. I don't really get it.

JONNY. I don't get what's not to get?

RACHEL. Are you annoyed?

JONNY. I'm confused, / that's all.

RACHEL. Have I done / something?

JONNY. Confused as to why you've gone shy all of a sudden?

RACHEL. I'm not shy.

JONNY. Thought you wanted to be a singer?

RACHEL. I never said that.

JONNY. What Billie said. Yous lot aren't the only ones that talk you know. If you're any good I'll write you a letter. 'Dear Simon.'

RACHEL. You're taking the piss.

JONNY. Am I?

RACHEL. –

JONNY. Go on.

Beat.

Rachel?

Beat.

No?

Long pause.

He gets up to leave.

RACHEL *starts singing – it might be 'Heaven Knows I'm Miserable Now' by The Smiths. It could be something else. It's worse than being naked.*

She cries furious, humiliated tears.

She stops singing before the end of the song.

Long pause.

RACHEL. I thought you were alright.

JONNY. No, I know what you thought. And you can tell them that I don't.

RACHEL. –

JONNY. Blame myself. I don't blame myself.

Blackout.

Scene Eight

Bathroom. BILLIE *washes her face over the sink.* RACHEL *stands in the doorway.*

RACHEL. Is it still bleeding?

Billie?

I can't really stay long.

BILLIE. I feel dizzy.

RACHEL. No, obviously I can stay for a bit but I just mean...

Do you want a sip of Coke? It's a bit warm but...

BILLIE. I'm gonna get a bruise.

RACHEL. Does it hurt?

BILLIE. Yeah.

RACHEL. I've never actually seen someone's nose get broken before.

BILLIE. You think it's broken?

RACHEL. Not yours. Ryan Dinnage's. Did you hear the noise it made? Like treading on a snail.

Beat.

Are you sure you're okay? I could get you some ice?

BILLIE. –

RACHEL. Have the Coke if you want. I'll get that...

RACHEL *exits.* BILLIE *turns around. Her bump is huge. There's blood on her T-shirt.*

Pause.

RACHEL *enters with a Vienetta.*

There wasn't any, I looked for peas or whatever but this was all I could... shall I wrap it in a towel or something?

BILLIE. Does it look like I'm getting a black eye?

RACHEL. No. A bit, maybe. Here then.

RACHEL *hands her the Vienetta.*

So. Will you be alright if I... Your dad'll be back soon, won't he?

BILLIE. He's getting a curry. To get the baby out. You might as well stay in case she comes.

RACHEL. I don't really like curry.

BILLIE. You can have something else.

RACHEL. My parents are taking me out to celebrate my results, all of us together. I think I actually did well better than they thought I was going to. My dad's gonna sleep at home tonight so... Oh, your results. You dropped them when it all kicked off.

She takes an brown envelope out of her bag, hands it to BILLIE.

Beat.

Aren't you gonna open them?

BILLIE. –

RACHEL. If it's cos you don't wanna tell me don't worry about it. I'm gonna bounce now anyway.

BILLIE. Bounce?

RACHEL. Yeah.

BILLIE. Keep your phone on.

RACHEL. I will.

BILLIE. It's any time from now. So you need to have it on loud.

RACHEL. Fine. I will.

BILLIE. Do it now. Put it on loud now.

RACHEL. Oh my god.

BILLIE. You didn't reply last night.

RACHEL. I was asleep.

BILLIE. What if that had been it? You'd have missed it.

RACHEL. Well, I didn't, did I.

BILLIE. What's your home number?

RACHEL. I'll make sure my mobile's on. Okay?

BILLIE. It could be tonight.

RACHEL. Yeah.

Beat.

Although, I've sort of made plans tonight.

BILLIE. Come here after.

RACHEL. I promised I'd go to Leah's party. It'll be shit, like I'm not really bothered about going but it's just... we might not see anyone from school ever again, do you know what I mean?

BILLIE. You'll see them at college.

RACHEL. Are you still...

BILLIE. What?

RACHEL. You're definitely going still?

BILLIE. Why wouldn't I?

RACHEL. No I just... you know. My mum said it was gonna be quite full-on. For the first bit.

BILLIE. I'm still going to college, Rachel.

RACHEL. Course.

Pause.

I'm sure you could come tonight? If you wanted?

BILLIE. Just keep your phone on.

RACHEL. I will. Defs. Deffo.

Beat.

The thing is. I'm not sure about the whole... Like if I can still make it.

BILLIE. Make it when?

RACHEL. It's not that, I'm just not sure if I can come. If I would be the best person.

BILLIE. For...

RACHEL. When you have her.

BILLIE. But you have to.

RACHEL. I'll try. Obviously.

BILLIE. You're my birthing partner. I put it on the forms.

RACHEL. I'm shit at stuff like that. Blood and... You'll be looking after me.

BILLIE. I'm having a baby, Rachel.

RACHEL. I know. It's just I can't like... guarantee... I just wanted to let you know. In case something comes up.

BILLIE. Like what?

RACHEL. It would be easier if you had more of an idea when she might come?

BILLIE. You can't order it, Rachel, it's not a Domino's.

RACHEL. Like, I'm going Thorpe Park this weekend, what if she comes then?

BILLIE. I can't go in on my own.

RACHEL. Your dad'll be there.

BILLIE. He hates hospitals.

RACHEL. Don't you have an auntie or something?

BILLIE. No. And I want you.

RACHEL. You'll be alright.

BILLIE. How do *you* know?

RACHEL. You'll be great. I know you will. And when you think about it... everyone that's ever lived, like ever, has been born, right? There's probably one just been born now. And another one now. And another one now –

BILLIE. I get it.

RACHEL. So it's not such a big deal when you think about it like that, is it?

BILLIE. It's a big as a watermelon.

RACHEL. It's the most natural thing in the world.

BILLIE. You said you cried when that boy from Year 12 put three fingers in.

RACHEL. So?

BILLIE. So imagine his fingers had a watermelon on the end.

RACHEL. I really want to be there –

BILLIE. Do you?

RACHEL. I do, you know I do. It's just… my mum. She's not sure, if it's a good idea. She thinks it might be…

BILLIE. What?

RACHEL. A bit much.

Beat.

Your nose is bleeding again.

BILLIE *bunches up a wad of tissue. Sticks it up her left nostril. The sound of the front door.*

I should go really.

BILLIE. Rachel? Ryan and… everyone. Why were they saying that stuff?

Beat.

RACHEL. I dunno.

JONNY *enters.*

JONNY. Mothers' meeting is it? Alright…

BILLIE. Rachel?

JONNY. Alright, Rachel?

RACHEL. Yeah.

JONNY. All go okay with your exams and that?

RACHEL. Yeah. Good. Better than I…

JONNY. Keeping busy are you?

Beat.

Good. Nice one. Billie? Wha's –

BILLIE. Nothing.

JONNY. Your face.

RACHEL. I'll get going.

JONNY. What's going on?

BILLIE. Nothing.

JONNY. The baby's alright?

BILLIE. She's fine.

JONNY. Well, what's happened?

Pause.

Come on, this ain't fair, you're fucking freaking me out here.

BILLIE. Don't swear, Dad.

JONNY. Rachel?

RACHEL. She headbutted a boy from school.

JONNY. You what?

BILLIE. I headbutted Ryan Dinnage.

JONNY. Who's Ryan Dinnage?

BILLIE. A boy from school.

JONNY. You went off right as rain this morning. I thought you was getting your results.

BILLIE. I was.

JONNY. And?

BILLIE. I dunno. I've not opened them.

JONNY. What you doing getting in fights?

BILLIE. He's a prick.

JONNY. Look at the state of you. You can't be fighting in the street.

BILLIE. It was in the car park.

JONNY. What will people be thinking?

BILLIE. It's not my fault.

JONNY. Nothing ever is, is it? Only you, Billie. Honestly. Bet none of the other girls was getting in fights. Was they, Rachel? You have a fight with anyone today?

RACHEL. No but –

JONNY. Course you haven't. But this one… Take that Sarah Lee off your face, that ain't gonna do anything.

BILLIE. It was Rachel's idea.

RACHEL. There aren't any peas.

JONNY crouches in front of BILLIE.

JONNY. Come on then. Let's have a look at you.

BILLIE. I'm fine.

JONNY. You shouldn't nut someone if you don't know how.

BILLIE. I made him cry.

JONNY. Nothing to be proud of, Bill. You bought her back, did you?

RACHEL. Yeah.

JONNY. Thanks for looking after her.

RACHEL. I didn't do anything.

Pause.

JONNY. Right. Well, get home safe. And yeah, thanks for taking care of Rambo here.

RACHEL. It's okay. Like I said… Bye then, Billie.

BILLIE. –

JONNY. Billie. Your mate's going.

RACHEL. And good luck okay, if I can't… You'll be amazing.

RACHEL *exits*.

JONNY. Well, there's a black eye coming. You bruise like a peach as it is. Come on then, Rocky, what was this fight about?

BILLIE. It was nothing.

JONNY. Are you being bullied?

BILLIE. No –

JONNY. You want me to have a word?

BILLIE. You'll make it worse.

JONNY. What's happened?

BILLIE. They were just… saying stuff.

JONNY. Like what?

BILLIE. About us.

JONNY. What?

Beat.

Not the car, is it?

BILLIE. No, not the car, Dad.

Pause.

JONNY. What about these results then?

BILLIE. I haven't yet.

JONNY. What you waiting for?

BILLIE. –

JONNY. Come on. I got Freud on the other line. He's worried you're after his job.

BILLIE. What if I haven't –

JONNY. Then it doesn't matter. It's bit of paper, Bill. Whatever it says we both know you're gonna do big wonderful things, okay?

BILLIE. 'Kay. After three then.

Beat.

BILLIE *and* JONNY. Three.

She rips the top off the brown envelope that RACHEL *gave her earlier. Blackout.*

Scene Nine

The bathroom. BILLIE *stands by the door. There's a shallow pool of water in the main bath. A baby-changing bag on the floor as well as a used nappy, Babygro, vest, etc.* FUDGE *is packing the used stuff into the bag.*

FUDGE. So?

BILLIE. –

FUDGE. What do you think?

BILLIE. –

FUDGE. Well, don't say right now, have a think about it.

BILLIE. Fudge…

FUDGE. What?

BILLIE. It's not right.

FUDGE. We've got a baby together.

BILLIE. You don't love me.

FUDGE. I do –

BILLIE. It's alright. I don't love you neither.

Pause.

FUDGE. So we need to decide.

BILLIE. On what?

FUDGE. On her name.

BILLIE. Oh.

FUDGE. Do you wanna give me your list first and I'll –

BILLIE. I don't have a list.

FUDGE. I'll tell you the ones I like.

BILLIE. You can choose.

FUDGE. Yeah? Okay, I liked Hope –

BILLIE. Really?

FUDGE. It's symbolic.

BILLIE. It's a bit…

FUDGE. I thought you didn't care.

BILLIE. I don't but… Hope. It's like calling her Lucky.

FUDGE. So you do care.

BILLIE. I just –

FUDGE. Mia?

BILLIE. –

FUDGE. I thought before you had her, like I was thinking about if it was a boy I'd wanna give him some hench name like Aslan or something but for a girl…. my nana was called Maria so I thought….

BILLIE. Mia.

FUDGE. Is it, do you mind?

BILLIE. Yeah.

FUDGE. Yeah you mind or –

BILLIE. Yeah whatever you think. You need to never have a son by the way. Aslan?

FUDGE. I don't get you, you know. I don't get how you don't wanna be with her all the time. Sometimes I wanna wake her up when she's asleep just cos I miss her. Can you believe that? How can you miss someone who's just there?

BILLIE. I don't know.

FUDGE. So?

BILLIE. So nothing.

FUDGE. Fuck's sake.

BILLIE. You weren't interested either, remember –

FUDGE. I was just... I was scared though a bit. And I still feel bad you know, about the way I treated you, both of you, but I'm trying to make it up. That's what I'm doing, Bill, I'm making it up to her.

Long silence.

She's proper dark, isn't she?

BILLIE. Yeah.

FUDGE. Everyone's saying she looks like I did. I was a cute baby, man.

BILLIE. –

FUDGE. Her personality is definitely you though. She flings her wrists around when she's sleeping like... (*Imitates boxing.*) Must've learnt that off your dad.

She doesn't laugh. He lights his cigarette. Silence. FUDGE *opens the window. Leans out to smoke.*

BILLIE. That's a nasty habit you know.

FUDGE. I'm trying to give up, but I got a lot of stress in my life at the moment, know what I mean?

Takes a few deep drags.

Adele's proper jealous.

BILLIE. Yeah?

FUDGE. Serious, she's needy at the moment always following me round like... She don't like sharing me I think.

BILLIE. It's not that I don't appreciate it. I do. And you were right. It was alright today, giving her a bath and that. But I still... You're good with her. She seems happy.

FUDGE. Try it. Just a couple of weeks, a month to start off with and if you don't like it you can move out. Come back here.

BILLIE. I can't, Fudge.

FUDGE. I had plans as well you know.

BILLIE. I know. I shouldn't have had her.

FUDGE. Billie! Why do you say things like that?

BILLIE. You just said you don't want her either.

FUDGE. I didn't want her. But she's here. She ain't goin' anywhere. She's actually well funny, the things she does. She don't even cry that much.

BILLIE. –

FUDGE. She needs a mum.

BILLIE. I was alright.

FUDGE. Your mum's dead, Bill, she isn't living round the corner.

Beat.

BILLIE. I've been looking at unis. Edinburgh, maybe like Oxford and stuff. My results were good so... What? What's funny?

FUDGE. Nothing.

BILLIE. You don't think I'm clever enough?

FUDGE. I don't think... You're not going Scotland, Billie, you pulled out of every school trip we ever had, there was some reason. You'll die here. In this oven. With him. Where is he anyways? Do I need to put on my fucking... bullet vest.

BILLIE. He's having a check-up.

FUDGE. His head I hope.

BILLIE. Arm. He's getting a big payout.

FUDGE. Right.

BILLIE. I'll give you money, for her stuff.

FUDGE. Fuck you.

BILLIE. I will.

FUDGE. Don't you love her?

Beat.

BILLIE. The thing is...

Beat.

She'll be alright with you. She thinks you're the shit already, imagine when you're giving lifts down the town and letting her eat peas off your plate. It will be better just the two of you.

FUDGE. We'll just go then shall we?

BILLIE. I am grateful.

FUDGE. You should be.

BILLIE. I am.

FUDGE. Right. Bye then.

BILLIE. Bye.

He doesn't move. Pause.

FUDGE. –

BILLIE. What?

FUDGE. Why you talking like you're not gonna see us again. We only live down the town.

The sound of a baby crying, off.

Do you mind?

BILLIE. Can't you?

FUDGE (*re: his fag*). Billie?

She doesn't move. He stubs out his cigarette, half-smoked on the sink. Exits. The baby's cries gets louder, then quieter, then stop. FUDGE re-enters with her in his arms.

Don't like being put down, do ya? She's proper lairy, Bill, you can tell already. Look at her face.

BILLIE goes close, stares at the baby. The baby starts crying again. BILLIE goes to the window, sticks her head out, breathes deeply. FUDGE rocks the baby vigorously till she stops crying.

What's wrong with you, man?

BILLIE. Don't.

FUDGE. You're nuts.

BILLIE. Don't joke.

FUDGE. You need to be careful. A bird might see that nose and think it's a nice juicy raspberry / swipe it right off.

BILLIE. Don't joke I said.

FUDGE. I'm not, you seen those seagulls?

Beat.

We actually do have to go. My auntie's picking us up.

BILLIE. Okay.

FUDGE. You're gonna think about what I said?

BILLIE. Yeah.

FUDGE. I know it's not perfect but… you can still do your college and uni and whatever you want. They wouldn't make us pay rent, I can work in the restaurant, save up, get a flat or something. They want us there. All of us. They're obsessed with her, Bill. With Mia. My dad would breastfeed her if he could I swear.

BILLIE. Your family are funny.

FUDGE. They like you.

BILLIE. Really?

FUDGE. Course they do. You're a fucking geek. Mum keeps going on at me to check up on you. Said you looked proper pale when she saw you in hospital.

BILLIE. I'm always pale.

FUDGE. And that you need a proper dinner. Fancy it?

BILLIE. What?

FUDGE. Come to mine for dinner.

BILLIE. I'm not a charity.

FUDGE. I can show you the baby's room and my mum can stuff you full of chicken.

BILLIE. I don't –

FUDGE. We'll give you a lift back tonight.

BILLIE. My dad looks after me really good. Tell your mum that.

FUDGE. Tell her yourself.

BILLIE. He's not…

FUDGE. What?

BILLIE. What everyone was saying at school. Ryan and… he's not like, weird.

FUDGE. You sure about that?

BILLIE. You know what I mean.

FUDGE. I know, Billie. I get it now okay?

Beat.

He'll be alright without you.

Pause.

BILLIE. Give me a minute.

FUDGE. Yes, Billie!

BILLIE. How long have I got?

FUDGE. I'll go down and tell her.

BILLIE. Okay.

FUDGE. Wait in the car. My mum's chicken is the nuts, Bill. You're gonna love it.

He slings the baby bag over one shoulder. Exits with the baby.

BILLIE *pauses*.

She exits and re-enters wearing trainers. She ties her hair back. Rinses out her mouth. Washes her face. She looks at herself for some time.

The sound of keys in the door.

JONNY (*off*). Bill?

Beat.

Billie?

*She takes the stub of the cigarette from the edge of the sink.
Puts it in her pocket.*

JONNY *enters.*

How you feeling?

BILLIE. Good.

JONNY. Promise?

BILLIE. Yeah.

JONNY. You look like you got a bit of colour back as it goes.

Beat.

Not gonna ask how it went?

BILLIE. Sorry. How'd it go?

JONNY. Very well thanks for asking.

BILLIE. What did she say?

JONNY. Yeah, yeah. Really good chance for the money I think.
Really good chance.

BILLIE. But is your shoulder okay?

JONNY. Yeah, no she thought it looked really bad. Gonna take
quite a bit longer to get the strength back, you know. I had to
tell her about that time I went fishing.

BILLIE. You've never been fishing.

JONNY. Course I have, I must have told you about that time.
When I went fishing. I caught a fish… and it was this big –
(*Flexes his muscles like Mr Universe, it's an old game.*)

BILLIE. Dad!

JONNY. And it bit me right here – (*Flexes his muscles down
pointing towards his bum.*)

BILLIE. You're so embarrassing, did you actually do that to the
doctor?

JONNY. Thought you loved that one.

BILLIE. I really don't.

JONNY. Right. Well… am I too embarrassing to sit next to on the sofa? Cos in my nifty little bag for life – I got DVDs. Girly ones. Popcorn, one of them smelly candles and a pair of steaks; doctor said you have to keep your iron up. So basically everything two girls could need for a massive night in. What do you reckon? Too embarrassing?

BILLIE. Maybe.

JONNY. Even if… (*Consults the DVD in the bag.*) Ryan Gosling is involved?

BILLIE. Maybe even then.

JONNY. Right, well I'd better –

The doorbell rings.

You expecting someone?

Beat.

Doorbell rings again.

Billie?

Beat

BILLIE. No.

JONNY. I'll go.

BILLIE. Probably selling something.

The bell rings again.

JONNY. Sure you're okay?

BILLIE. Yeah.

JONNY. You didn't have plans already?

BILLIE. Why d'you say that?

Long pause.

Looks like rain, anyway.

JONNY. Right. I'll get this film on then, shall I. It's a choice of *La La Land* or *How to Lose a Guy in Ten Days*. They both look fucking terrible.

BILLIE. *Scarface* it is then.

JONNY. Right. And you can take your shoes off, babe. We ain't going anywhere.

He exits.

A beat.

Then she quietly closes the door, locks it.

She goes to the window and looks out.

The faint sound of a car pulling away.

She dips her hands in the baby's bath water. Drinks a little from her hands.

She gets JONNY*'s lighter from a tin beside the toilet. Takes* FUDGE*'s cigarette stub out her pocket.*

Goes back to look out the window.

Lights the cigarette.

Pulls the plug in the bath.

She is still.

Blackout except for the orange of the fag.

Then black.

End.

www.nickhernbooks.co.uk

facebook.com/nickhernbooks

twitter.com/nickhernbooks